Life Had Other Plans

AMY LAURENS

OTHER WORKS

KADITEOS
How Not To Acquire A Castle

SHARDS OF FATE
Touchstone

STORM FOXES
A Fox Of Storms And Starlight
A Stag Of Snow And Memory

SHORTER WORKS
All The Things We Saved You From
Bones Of The Sea
Christmas Miracle Is Just A Saying
Dreaming of Forests
Mint Grows Even In The Dark
Rush Job
Trust Issues

COLLECTIONS
And Then I Shall Transform
April Showers
Cherry Blossom And Other Stories
Darkness And Good
It All Changes Now
Of Sea Foam And Blood
The Inklet Collection

POETRY & PLAYS
Change Becomes Us
For A Little While
Life Had Other Plans
Where Your Treasure Is

NON-FICTION
How To Write Dogs
How To Theme
How To Create Cultures
How To Create Life
How To Map
How To Plan A Pinterest-Worthy Party Without Dying
On The Origin Of Paranormal Species
The 32 Worst Mistakes People Make About Dogs

FOR YOUNGER READERS

SANCTUARY
Where Shadows Rise
Through Roads Between
When Worlds Collide

The Ice Cream Crown Skating Races

Find more about the author:
www.AmyLaurens.com

LIFE HAD OTHER PLANS

AMY LAURENS

AUSTRALIA

Copyright © 2025 Amy Laurens

All rights reserved. No part of this book may be reproduced in any form or by any electronic or mechanical means, including information storage and retrieval systems, without permission in writing from the publisher, except by a reviewer, who may quote brief passages in a review.

This is a work of fiction. All characters, organisations and events are the author's creation, or are used fictitiously.

Without in any way limiting the author's exclusive rights under copyright, no part of this book may be used or reproduced in any manner for the purpose of training artificial intelligence (AI) technologies or systems without express contractual permission from the author.

Paperback ISBN: 978-1-923305-09-0
eBook ISBN: 9798230425960

www.inkprintpress.com

National Library of Australia Cataloguing-in-Publication Data
Laurens, Amy 1985—
Life Had Other Plans
92 p.   cm.
ISBN: 978-1-923305-09-0
Inkprint Press, Canberra, Australia
1. Poetry—Women Authors 2. Poetry—Australian & Oceanian 3. Poetry—Subjects & Themes—Motivational & Inspirational

Summary: Poetry about surviving life's curve balls with grace and dignity.

First Edition: May 2025

Cover design © Inkprint Press.
Cover image via Canva.com under commercial licence

CONTENTS

Dedication 9

Life Had Other Plans 10
A Homecoming 13
It's A Choice, Really 14
You Are The Fire That Forged My Bones 16
Once More Into The Breach 18
I Am Grounded, And That Is Fine 19
An Apology Of Sorts 22
The Agony Of Not Writing 23
Come To Bed, Love 24
An Ode To The Humble Raspberry 26
Christmas Day 28
Some Things Are Still Worth Doing 30
We The Pigs 31
Oxidation 32
When Life Is Hard And Uninspiring 34
Surely 36
Then Life Had *Other* Other Plans 38
Transformation 41
Cancer Is Only A Lens 43
Machines Are Not So Brittle 46
An Ode To The Poems Lost While
    Reaching For My Phone 48
A Cycle Ending 51

My Soul Is Starving, Even As
    My Body Is Fed 53
A Slightly Cheesy Haiku 56
There Are Fireflies In My Bones
    And White Gold In My Soul 57
On Waiting Patiently For The Miracle
    I Know Is Coming 60
Prophecy Is A Moonstone 63
Survivor's Guilt 65
In The Middle Of The Air 67
Tomorrow Vs. Today 68
Rebirth Is Inevitable 70
Poems And Oceans Both Encircle
    The World 72
The Value We Attribute 74
Weltschmerz II 76
Because Stories Matter 78
Sorrow Is Not Inherently Greater 81
Decompression 83
A Translation From Gif To Poetry, From
    Gifs Arranged In Response To Poetry 85
A Conclusion Of Sorts 87

DEDICATION

I
I have loved you all my life,
or at least as much of it as fits
between now and the moment
you first put Pratchett in my hands.

II
You are the bestie
I never expected to have and
that makes the surprise all the more
wonderful, like a $50 note left
in the pocket of your winter coat.

LIFE HAD OTHER PLANS
Spring 2023

Today feels like
a good day to write
a poem, and
that is strange, because
I had other plans.

I did not expect this year
the slow decline
down a gently sloping mountain
of verdant green grass,
into a flat-bottomed valley filled
with the deep river of oblivion,
obscured by fog.
That was never in the outline.
That was never the itinerary.
But life had other plans.
(It always does.)

Out my window is a citrus tree:
it might qualify as topiary if
it were just a little less
free
form.
Shoulder-high, in a beige-glazed
pot, it was supposed to be a
gift of cumquats, fresh

fruit in season hanging
like topaz
earrings
amid
glossy-leaved hair;
Alack. The tree is a calamondin,
identical
in appearance but
bitter
in fruit.
Life, it seems, had other plans.

Below the pot, eight yellowed
leaves curl on the patio tiles,
the last scars of the tree's battle
with hail, some four-and-change
months ago, finally discarded—
like growth.
Like healing.
Like life had other plans
for this tree than death by assault
from the sky.

I love everything, today, my current
view included:
Roses! I love roses!
Tea! I love tea!
My journal! I love my journal!
Dog walkers! I love dog walkers!
Poetry! Don't mind if I do!

What I really love is this:
Having shed the yellowed scars of
assault-by-elemental-force,

12

I can once again see the sky,
and it is blue.
Cerulean.
I didn't dare assume today
would see such steep contrast
to yesterday's overcast skies.
But life
had other plans.

A HOMECOMING

It seems I have once more veered
sharply
off the cliffs of fiction into the ocean
of poetry, a circular, periodic coming home
like the rhythmic motion of the waves my
heart seeks to crash against
the shoreline of
certitude, seeking expansion, seeking growth,
the growth of the ocean that erodes
the cliffs of certainty whereon
false identities are founded; although
I long to write fiction by the reams until
the blood of it drips from my lips and my
fingers, staining everything I touch with
narratives of what it means to be
human, to strive, to reach, to grasp, to yearn,
yet I circle back just now to wash
the lint from my thinking and to
dip again into the salt of poems that
lick the detritus from between my toes like
waves caressing their beloved, connecting
shore with shore despite the distance and
bathing us all in the aquamarine beauty
of the womb.
Sometimes, falling
off a cliff
just means coming home.

IT'S A CHOICE, REALLY

It bemuses me that
my brain has decided this
is the space for thinking when
it is constantly cluttered and
fighting for breath, crammed
between the kitchen and the office, currently
covered in folded white sheets, a
blue quilt my mother sewed me,
precisely two books (presents for an
impending birthday), my dark
blue journal and metallic mint
pencil case, a teal teapot limned with tea and
a matching teacup with dregs pooling in
the bottom and the last two
pockey sticks that somehow made their
way here from Korea and a pile
of seed husks from the purple kale, their
stalks like chopsticks thrown asunder after
the meal is done and
a bright red box cutter for cutlery and
a box of copper-coloured screws and
a discarded grey jumper as a dinner guest and
a handwritten list of incomplete chores on
half a torn scrap of paper and
a new phone box with a white charging cable stretching
the width of the dining table and
plants in beige and black and grey and white pots
creating a little forest at the far end, though

one of the pots is pink because it's
mine and there's medicine
for the smallest child and
salt for everyone's dinner and
a discarded mask turned blue side in and
sunscreen and a plastic cup and
me because
somehow in all of this cluttered
detritus of our cluttered
lives my mind has decided that
here is a spot I can create.
So long as there is room to push things
aside for my laptop to
balance at the edge of the table and
so long as there is room enough for me to
sit with one foot dangling
toward the floor,
there's room enough for poetry.
Oh,
and a strip of nails for the nail gun.

YOU ARE THE FIRE THAT FORGED MY BONES

You suck
all the air from the room like
a fire bent on burning
pretence from my bones as
excuses fall to ash in
your presence.
I will be conquered, or
I will burn and emerge
standing,
a phoenix scorched home to
myself.
My bones are steel. They are
a good frame on which to build
a new home, now that the old
one has been swept away in the
tidal flood of your assault, teaching
me what it means to have
strong enough foundations
to withstand the storm of your
presence.
I do not regret this.
Fire-forged bones made
of steel, clothed with flood-strong,
storm-proof muscle?
I could never but thank
you for that

even if I did feel
like I was suffocating
while you were here.

ONCE MORE INTO THE BREACH

Once more into the breach, dear friends
we go and the breach is not
a hammered-down gaping hole
in the wall that separates friend
from foe
but rather the opportune moment
that seeks to restore two halves
of one whole
to unity.
Thus is the purpose of poetry,
at least for me.
The breach of which we speak is
entirely internal and
entirely unnecessary and
entirely fictional, which of course
doesn't mean it isn't true.
My self has been breached, and
to counter this, I must become
myself.
For reasons as yet unknown,
poetry
is the mortar my subconscious
chooses
to reinforce myself.

I AM GROUNDED, AND THAT IS FINE

Burnout
is not about my context or
my surroundings
but about the whirling, swirling
chaos of the infinite
inside.
The seed of self doubt can be watered
and, with time,
blossom into an apple tree like
none ever seen before,
a variety all its own,
unique,
laden with empathy and
compassion for the world
and for my soul.

I am grounded.
My feet are rooted in the ground.

Like a sunflower, I bend up
ward to face the sun
and am blessed
by the knowledge
that I am enough.
I make decisions from this place, empowered,
and my quest for efficiency is a blessing that

I can choose to utilise or not,
as it serves me.
I am not a slave to efficiency. Not
in my body, and not
in my mind.
My mind is not a slave to anyone;
this is a salve.

I am grounded.

There is a perfect way to do things and
there is an efficient way to do things and
neither of them are the right way because
the right way is human.
Perfection is for the divine,
efficiency for the machine.
Instead, we are blessed to be a combine of the two.
I dance between these paths, lightly,
a hummingbird of agility, suckling from
flowers that serve me best in the moment,
and I am well.

I will be successful
and it will be in my own time
and on my own terms
and I have wisdom to offer the world that costs
me nothing, and
that is fine.

I am grounded.

Things are not valued by their expense.
Even cheap wisdom can prove wise.
I am not required to bleed

to prove my authenticity.
Airy words can land as softly in the heart
as blood.

And I am grounded.
That is fine.

I hunger.
And that is fine.

AN APOLOGY OF SORTS

I wasn't born
to be a careful poet,
crafting words meticulously
for years on end.
Instead, my words spill
carelessly,
rough-cut stones that
sometimes
house diamonds,
spilling from my mouth
like breath that spirals
away into the air until
it turns into leaves discarded
in the autumn sun,
some deeply veined with crimson,
laced with butter-yellow,
beautiful and restorative to behold,
while others fall dry
and crunchy and nut-brown to the ground
(though to be fair, even things crunchy
and nutty can be good on toast).
Some geodes contain gems;
some only disappointing rock—
or least, rock that's disappointing
if you were expecting gems.

A geologist, I expect, would see the
value regardless.

THE AGONY OF NOT WRITING

My heart is so full
of the world that it
is leaking out my eyes,
and I do not mean this
in the way that you expect.

For once, the wellspring
of these tears is not the
soul-crushing horrors of
humanity—nay, say not
humanity, for I truly
do believe that to be human
is to love.

And, for a wonder, that
is now the wellspring of
this fullness that seeps
out from me: an awe too
great to contain, too
large to hold on, too
vast to conceive—
and I am here to pin
it to the page

And I am not.

COME TO BED, LOVE

Come to bed, love,
and dream sweet comfort beneath
feathers magic in their transmutation
from something light and airy
to the weight of down reminding me
where my limbs belong.

Come to bed, love,
and dream of better days when
renovations no longer plague our
waking thoughts and plasterboard
no longer serves as entree for the
rabbit (we assume she likes the texture,
not the taste).

Come to bed, love,
and dream of peaceful things,
of star-spangled skies and
truths writ large against the body
of the earth, brown with love,
green with delight, of featherlight joy
and hot air balloons to buoy us
far away from sorrow.

Come to bed, love,
and dream, for in that dreaming lies
a truth your heart wants to divine,
and it will unfurl from the depths

of your soul like feathered, fern-frond wings
to soar through nights both bleak and bright,
where stars are seen or no,
where shadows skulk or caress,
to where your soul roams free.

For these dreams hunger,
as your bed hungers for you
and the lateness of the hour
hungers
for my slumber.
Come to bed, love,
sleep is calling to us both
and my soul,
it longs to dream.

AN ODE TO THE HUMBLE RASPBERRY

...is a misnomer to start with, for
who could argue that the raspberry,
with its gleaming red drupelets and
silver-backed leaves is humble? To me,
the most opulent of fruit, true
decadence against the lips, the cunning
way it fits against the tip of your
tongue like a protective secret;
the raspberry is certainly not humble.
And yet, gleaming ruby-like in golden
afternoon sunlight that hangs like
honey in the air, the raspberry is a
genteel fruit, much more aristocratic
than the loganberry that sprawls
drunkenly off its trellises, vines weaving
and crawling and creeping, invading the
raspberry patch like the handsy,
unwelcome bar mate that it is, small thorns
catching and clutching and cursing.

No. The gallant raspberry offers its fruits
on fronds bethorned yet delicate,
each one a friendly, waving arm bending low
to offer a heady cluster of gleaming jewels
that slide right off the bush as easily
as doffing a hat. Leaf-green shield beetles

stand guard over waving fronds like
courtiers assembling in a ruby-encrusted
palace, and the tiny hairs on the raspberry's
chin are so easily forgiven, lending an air of
distinguishment rather than being unkempt.
As these gleaming jewels mound up in
bowls and buckets and Tupperware too lowly
for such a well-mannered fruit, I am reminded
of the only fault such a gem possesses:
that, now plucked from the bush, its lifespan is
but momentary before gleaming drupelets
turn to mush.

Then again, perhaps this is chief amongst
its virtues: the fruit itself practically demands
we cram it in by the handful until our mouths
bleed red, hunger never quite satiated for this
most genteel of fruits.

CHRISTMAS DAY

Silver-white clouds overcast-
ing shadows into green-bright grass,
tarnished silver minky
weighting the bed in which
I am cocooned;
a late afternoon hibernation
tasting of creaming soda and grilled peaches while
children play merrily outside,
silvered light filtering through slatted blinds
to silver-leafed walls bedecked with
oriental paintings and a sailboat,
sleepy thoughts and silvered eyelids
heavy with the weight of happiness and repose,
flavoured by long conversations and
silver baubles on twisted branches that adorn the
heavily laden outdoor table, bowing under the weight
of gleaming jewelled salads and brushed gold
potatoes and merriment of things long past.
Selfishly, I have abandoned my companions
to the wet air and warmth
in favour of my cocoon
where cool-conditioned air breathes crystalline
against my cheeks.

Later, we emerge, and hie ourselves
to the coast where the
silvered sky shivers with spitted rain, salt and the
shushing of the tide flowing in, a soft

background of blurred movement, water
colour, blues and grey,
characters oil-painted bright
and vivid, sharp edged on the
sharp edges of the tide pool rock.
A rotating roster of grinning dogs,
some black as sea urchins,
some tan as the ocean stone.
People swap in and out, hair
tawny and sandy and honey-gold,
skin sun-tanned and star-kissed and toasted,
suits sea-grass green and summer-sky cyan,
wetsuits seal-black and flippers fish-yellow,
waving aloft flags like fins.
The gentle sway and dance as people shift
in and out, in and out,
drifting on a human tide as the water ebbs slowly
away.

We finish the day with tables rich in left-
overs, sating ourselves on wilting peach salads and
rosemary-roasted potatoes now slightly
past their peak, but beloved all the more
for the memories they hold of a time
not yet long past
but nevertheless relegated now to story, to be
repeated oft into the future, this time when
we harkened together from different corners
of the globe to celebrate, give thanks,
and together find our fill.

SOME THINGS ARE STILL WORTH DOING

There is nothing much
to be said
about love
that has not been
said before,
but there is nothing much
to live
of love
that has not been lived before
either.

WE THE PIGS

The world is heavy as a sack
of bricks and
the only thing it is good
for is knocking sense into
the heads of so-called 'leaders'
who think only of their own
foundations and care not
for who else's homes they may
destroy in their pursuit,
but I have not the strength
to wield this bag of bricks
as it ought be wielded, for
I am not the Big Bad Wolf;
that is the ones who
appropriate
the strength of the people in order
to build strongholds for themselves,
wherein they sit sipping tea and
eating fresh bread while
outside, stale cake languishes and
we the pigs hammer at their door
shouting, You're murdering our brothers,
please stop.

OXIDATION

How fitting it is that
death exists
as an extant form of beauty,
which appears so soft and
inviting, like I could
caress its golden tongues and
stroke its scarlet sparks as the
blue-hearted, flickering flames
flare ever upward.
How fitting it is that death,
the extant form of beauty that it is,
is also searing, heat intense and
burning, melting flesh from
bone and pretence from the
soul, at least for those who
brush against it.
How fitting, as it pops and
crackles here beside me,
no sound other than the
keys of my computer to
accompany it, that death
should glow enticingly,
embers warm and useful
for alchemy
or cooking
or transmutation
or simply warmth.

Even the charcoal left behind is
good for making soil,
treasured by helpful bacteria as
a new hearth in which to grow that
makes fertile barren soils and
cleanses all manner of things.
It even absorbs toxins.
Strange, perhaps, that of
all natural things, it is death
we find most beautiful.
Strike it up in the middle of the
emptiest field,
and all are drawn to its flame.
We make friends as we sit around it.
We laugh, and sing, toast
marshmallows in the liminal spaces
between air and flame, flame and air.
We tell stories.
By the soothing, homey light
of death,
we are human.

As I'm sure you are familiar,
we're all burning
slowly
on the inside.

WHEN LIFE IS HARD AND UNINSPIRING

The scene out the window might,
if one were feeling so uninspired,
be considered dreary. Silvery over
cast skies shadow damp, bedraggled
grass and
raspberry leaves are withering on the
canes and the pear is turning autumn
yellow even though by the calendar
it's winter. (Just.)
Soggy mud and dripping grey eaves,
the coriander bushes bowed down by
drizzle and
the bright red ladder the only
spot of colour in the yard.
Even the pink-flowering camellia
seems half asleep today.
The trampoline is a wet mirror of the
sky, its black skin silvered;
the pumpkin vines are shrivelled on
the chicken's playpen fence.
Tomatoes cant in dying slumber;
even the seed heads of the purple dragon
carrots have turned dun.
Lemons shiver on the shrub and
oranges quiver in the cold and
something has stripped the foliage from

the chard, its yellow ribs stretching
skyward like pleading fingers, begging
for mercy
and respite.
And yet...
And yet.
This dreary scene, at first brush
uninspiring, is in fact the very
opposite:
Witness here this poem as my proof.

SURELY

The absurdity that is the
chain of consequences that is:
- perform random Google search
- discover random YouTube channel
- like and subscribe
- search up their book and

ONE DAY LATER,
- sit in the afternoon sun
sipping mint tea and
reading the book with the blue cover that
arrived that morning that
you hadn't heard of
the morning before, while

AT THE SAME TIME
a consequential chain exists that is
- wake up to discover that
your country is at war and
- you must evacuate only
- there is nowhere to evacuate to and
- the bombs are falling on
the place that's supposed to be
safe and

SO FEW DAYS LATER
perhaps you are the only one to survive from
- your family and
- your friends and
- your community and

the world is a glass marble whose

surface is sliced by multitudinous reflections and
none of these experiences negate the other but
surely if we can invent
same-day shipping we can
stop the bombs from falling.

THEN LIFE HAD *OTHER* OTHER PLANS
Winter 2024

When I said
that life had other plans
I also did not expect a
dresser bedecked with blushing roses,
dusky pink lisianthus and neon-bright gerberas,
a scented bouquet of Erlicheer jonquils
perfuming my nightstand like
delicate, beautiful complexity in their
sage-painted tall Ball jar.

I did not expect a brown paper bag
on the floor by my bed, well
crinkled and well
loved for the treasure trove of white-boxed
medicine it contains, whose function
for now is
keeping me alive, until
my poor neglected body can one day
do that all by herself again.

I did not expect an outpouring of
love and affection, such as I have never
seen before, all directed at me, the one who I
but recently believed
to be an inconvenience.

(Perhaps I still believe this, but
I'm learning that to be loved
is to be an inconvenience of choice,
and in a world where free will is
more precious than any currency, perhaps
it is time for me to stop playing
the bank among my friends.)

I did not expect three-hour drives and
twenty-three-hour plane flights and
thirty-three hours of phone calls and
messages and prayers and the Spirit of God
rippling through the air and through my soul,
unteasing all these final knots that
keep me small and
have done all my life.
I am Gordian, yet I will be untied.

I did not expect cancer, because no one
ever does, and I did not expect it to feel
like this,
like love, like life, like a transparent window
into the soul-deep goodness of the world,
the mirror to the one who made it,
sustainer of all things and bringer of
consciousness and life.
I should have known by now that
truth nests in ironies and builds
its home in sparrow-feathered paradoxes far
more often than in simple maxim or adage.

I did not expect any of this, any more
than I expected a sky: cerulean.
Life, of course, had other plans,

and as it transpires, all the blues
of the sky
are beautiful
in their moment.

TRANSFORMATION

The taking of dust and transforming it
into rain as it spirals through
the air gathering moisture until it
finally has sufficient mass to
fall
is often how I feel about
my writing. A pregnancy,
a seeding, a period of gathering into
myself all thoughts and ideas and
dusty concepts necessary to create
the stew and slurry of creativity that
gives birth to rain-like words,
drenching pages with love and
nourishment and life.
I am pregnant now, or am growing
so at least, ideas cross-pollinating and
fertilising within as they
clatter and clash and spiral and whirl until
eventually—I hope—something beautiful
births.
I have felt this way before, standing
on the precipice
of a torrent of words ready to
sweep me away and scour the
pretence from my bones and
bring the whole wide world along
with me for the ride as we cling
together wildly to our lashed-up logs,

screaming madly to the sky with
unbridled delight as lightning splits
above us and thunder rattles our
preconceptions and we slide to the end
of the river as new-birthed from our
mothers—and yet those times, the
birthing never came.
This time, as I pick away at liminal spaces
that outline projects I have loved for
years, their seams stitched into the soft-worn
corners of my smile, and
gently mother them into a more fulsome
existence…
This time, I hope the rains will come.
When they do, they will bless us all.

CANCER IS ONLY A LENS

Cancer is only a thief if
we assume that's how
this story ends.

It doesn't.

It doesn't end here.

And so, with that in mind,
armed with the knowledge
that the ending determines
the theme and the
important parts of the story
are the lessons the main
characters learn along the way,
perhaps in this time,
in this moment,
in this iteration of 'now',
cancer is merely a lens.

When my son was born,
my husband insisted
it changed nothing.
I was outraged.
It clearly changed
everything.

But he insisted: it was
only a lens. Clarifying.
Refining. Stripping
away everything
unnecessary until only
that which was important
remained.

Cancer is the child I
never planned to adopt,
and yet here I am with this
new lens filtering my life,
clarifying my priorities,
refining my needs hour by
hour and stripping away
everything unnecessary until
only that which is vital
remains.

I always had too many plans.
As I wipe the sparkling tear spilling
from your cheek with a gentle
fingertip, I urge you now not
to give in to the dark: that was
not prescience. My anxiety has
never been the best part of me,
so do not let it stand in for future
knowledge or for foresight, else
I'd have never seen a family
member again after they left my
sight and anxiety insisted they
were gone forever.

My frenetic spiralling of 'must
do this' and 'must do that' was
not borne of any special insight
about the length of my life; it
was just anxiety, and we all
know anxiety lies.

This is the lens that clarifies.

Now I am forced to decide.

What *will* I do with this
one, precious, wild
life I'm given?

MACHINES ARE NOT SO BRITTLE

I am not, of course, a
machine, because if I
were then I would
deconstruct myself,
teasing out every fibre of
my innermost being into
something countable,
sortable, parseable, a
pile of disparate pieces
able to be catalogued and
identified, things with
specific roles and jobs and
the ability to define if they
were 'working'
or if not.

Instead, my innermost
soul is infinite, unknowable,
and I have a body capable
of doing things like
building children
out of nothing
and invading my sacred
space with mutant cells,
entirely unbeknownst to me,
and this miracle of

unknowingness is
horrifying.

No microscopic analysis
helps when it's
your own inside you
wish to assess.

Am I well? Is it
growing?
I am not a machine.
And this is brittle.

AN ODE TO THE POEMS LOST WHILE REACHING FOR MY PHONE

An ode to all words
so perfect and pristine, formed
in the darkness of the pre-sleep
night, womblike in its
fertility.
Now, as I lay me down to
sleep, all thoughts and
glorious ideas come,
gliding in to fill the empty
spaces of the day, liminal,
delicious, satiating.

And yet, with no way to
memorise them fully to
ensure their survival until
dawn, I reach for phone to
pin them gently into place,
butterflies with gilded wings,
beetles with iridescent chiton,
dragonflies that dart on
transparent wings in the dark,
and as my hand clutches the
cool, sleek sides of my device,
insectly thoughts flee as though

I have shone an unwelcome
spotlight
on them, and are gone

and I am left wondering
whether this is an
inevitability of life and
the way that creative thought
works, or if it is something more
sinister at bay, a sneaky form
of self-sabotage wherein jewel-like
bugs are conjured only
when they feel they are safe
from any danger of entrapment;
is it in the nature of insects to
proliferate in the quiet, gentle
dark, or is it instead a product
of some deeper fear that seeks
to shield beauteous creatures
from any possible critical eye?

Surely, such gems deserve
better than to dissipate like
fog or airy words or steam,
hauntingly into the night.
Surely, such charming bugs
with deep green-black and
purple-blue and orange-pink
to their shimmering
deserve a daytime space as well,
capacious and plentiful,
roomy and airy enough to
take flight so that they may
find a page to land on and

thus endure forever.

One must, I think, respect
such things, if one wishes
not to lose all poems
to the dark.

A CYCLE ENDING

For nigh on thirty years my life has been
ruled by rhythms seemingly unchanged:
the loss of blood four-weekly, less two days,
accompanied by several days of pain.

I thought I'd made the choice to end this cycle—
a decision based on pain, discomfort, cramps—
and celebrated when I thought my last
time through this cycle had arrived, then passed.

Control was wrested from me then, however,
by cancer's sudden twisting of my plot;
the cancellation of procedures longed for,
now substituted by a set of shots.

Eventually I'll bleed no more regardless,
but one more time I'm forced now to confront it:
this time is much more messy, much more real,
underestimating how I'd feel.

It was one thing when the choice was fully mine,
when I was choosing when and where and why,
but forgoing menstrual cups this time has brought
me face to face with agency denied.

Red spirals down the drain and's washed away;
I would my feelings were as quickly quelled.
Instead I have inside me here a raging,

seething mess of resentment and
confusion and regret for
a choice I'd already made
regardless.

I did not expect that
grief would find me
so easily when
last month
I'd been
cele
bra
ti
 n

   g.

MY SOUL IS STARVING, EVEN AS MY BODY IS FED

I stumbled last night, stubbing
my fingers against an old blog I
haven't visited in years, like a
friend I haven't seen since uni,
the slightly awkward, uncomfortable
joy of wrapping your arms
around the neck of someone
they haven't quite forgotten
how to embrace, and now
I am drowning in the colour
of an overcast sky dragging
me down into something that
looked like a small puddle,
barely the size of my gumboot,
but which turned out to be
a vast lake where, sinking
to the sandy, seaweedy bottom,
the pressure of all that water
is crushing my chest and
stealing away
my breath.

It was a cooking blog I
used to run with a friend,

and nostalgia tastes like
watermelon feta cupcakes that
didn't turn out so well but
also like the plum-passionfruit
ones I'd make again in a heartbeat
if they didn't take so long
and that is at least half of the
problem, which is that I no longer
have space in my life—*had*
space in my life—to experiment
in ways that light me up like a
bubble of golden, glowing light,
buoyant enough to rise even
from the darkest, deepest lake.

The other fifty percent, of course,
is that my life has been a study
in the slow whittling away of
everything I like to eat, stolen
from me by a body too broken
to process food like a normal
person would, too intolerant
to allow me my personal pleasures,
stripping the skin back on my
joy until something pale and raw
remains, and the cancer has only
made it worse, stealing from me
the last few joyful foods I knew.

Once, I loved cooking enough to
dedicate entire days to play and
experimentation and carved a
dedicated space for documentation.

Now, I hate food with such a passion
that if it weren't for the nausea and
passive listless dying that accompanies,
I'd simply choose never
to eat again.

A SLIGHTLY CHEESY HAIKU

I had no idea
how much it was possible
to think about cheese.

THERE ARE FIREFLIES IN MY BONES AND WHITE GOLD IN MY SOUL

For Kerryn, with love and gratitude

It is a marvel of technology
that makes cancer look
so beautiful: golden sparks
aflame throughout my
skeleton, burning bright and
beautiful as I spin in three dimensions,
directed by the drag
of forefinger against
my phone screen.

Lavender skeleton, firefly
sparks where bones are busy
degrading, or else frantically repairing,
causing them to suck thirstily
of the phosphate dye
injected into my veins
several hours ago.

I cannot stop watching it,
entranced by the spinning of
my ribs and
pelvis and
spine,

the fire-orange glow that
flecks the bones, fading in from
lavender, magenta, fire-engine red
until suddenly, a burst of white-gold
coruscating through my lumbar
vertebrae and sacroiliac joint,
and you tell me that this is
thing of holy beauty
(and it is)
and you tell me that this light is
where my body communes
with the magic of the universe,
accreting miracles that fall
like dust motes sparkling
in a beam of light, where
the friction of my soul
rubs up against eternity
and finds entrance to
the third path I agreed to
that leads me to
my dreams.

Technology is a miracle
that lights this horrible,
sacred, intimidating path,
and the road to my dreams
is lit by fireflies
that gleam inside my bones,
bearing me to eternity on
their wings.

(A good thing fireflies
fly slowly, lest eternity
come too quick.)

I should have known that
I'd not be asked to walk
the dark alone; fireflies are
seen best after nightfall,
after all.

ON WAITING PATIENTLY FOR THE MIRACLE I KNOW IS COMING

In one simple phrase you
have calmed all the fears
of my restless, uncertain
heart. Where I seek
certainty like a cliff face
to dive from, conviction
as a nest from which I might
fly, conclusive confidence as
the DNA that knits together
the daily optimism of my
soul, my circumstances now
have cut me off from clarity,
curdling within me any sense
of calm that instinctively I
want to burrow into like
cotton-wool clouds, silver and
grey and cosy and warm, a
fog wherein it is easy to believe
the best of life, because I cannot
see how far away the ground is.

Irony, that the calm I call clarity
is actually cotton-wool oblivion.
Regardless, I cannot have it,

and that has clawed at my heart
today, ripping it to shreds as I
bleed crimson in search of the
solid foundation I crave. You,
however, have gifted me the
magic talisman I didn't know
I needed, the words to soothe
my fractious soul:
"The flame is not yet kindled
But there is time yet for it to catch."

Just because I cannot reach out
and touch right now the ephemeral
wings of the miracle I know is
coming—

Last year, I waited on another
miracle, and was reminded by
one who saw me well
that to wait well on a miracle
is not to nag. —

And so. There is time yet
for it to catch,
and in the meantime,
I will not waste time
with incessant nagging.

The cotton wool is stripped away,
and I can see the ground,
and the oaks and eucalypts
and sycamores and pines
are tiny and immeasurable and
I cannot see clearly enough to judge

when the ground will near
and that is the point.

I will not waste the time
with incessant nagging.
My children have taught me well
how exhausting that is for
everyone, and how little
it's likely to succeed.

PROPHECY IS A MOONSTONE

Prophecy is a moonstone,
which when worn the wrong
way is nothing but a bit
of white stone, relatively
unremarkable, practically
common, and the dullness
of it hurts
as though it were obsidian
sharp enough to carve
into your very soul, tracing
lines of grief and sorrow and
if you are unlucky, also
regret.

But prophecy is a moonstone,
which when worn the right
way glimmers iridescent blue
in the morning light, entirely
magical, practically
a miracle, and the intensity
of its shine transports
as though it were a portal
to another life, breathing
hope into your very soul,
inflating a tide of joy and
peace and, if you are very

lucky, inspiration too.

Prophecy is just another word
for prognosis and
like a hologram, two
realities can be true
at once.

SURVIVOR'S GUILT

Attending a funeral
while wearing a terminal diagnosis
is a weighty thing indeed,
especially when I fully intend
to shuck that diagnosis like
a coat I'd worn for winter,
no longer needed once bright sunlight
returns to my world with its
warmth, and light, and healing.

But that too is a weighty thing,
because here I sit in rows of hundreds
as we mourn together the life of
someone marvellous and the
grace, and poise, and dignity
of his widow—such an aging word,
a cruel word, a diminishing word—
pierces my heart, and we all
pound Providence together as we
ask where miracles reside for this
family, in this time;
Who am I to cling to mine?

Honestly, I see why people give
up. To accept my prognosis
would be to accept certainty;
an ugly, awkward, sharp-stabbing
rock to stand on with bare feet,

but a rock nevertheless. Instead,
I am choosing still to free fall through
a wild, rushing nothing that might
be grace and might be simply
delusion;
there is no way to know until the
fall is over.

In the meantime, all around me,
small certainties—some joyful,
some that shatter lives—and I
am drowning as I try to remember
that certainty does not correspond
to correctness.

I've no clue who I am,
to cling with such hubris to
faith/delusion; I've no clue why
others are not permitted the same and
my chest is broken open too for
this woman of grace and dignity and
loyalty and friendship and I
have insufficient words to draw her
in your mind, but I love her and
my heart is burst like an over-squeezed
water balloon and yet
it does no good to cast
my miracle aside simply because others
were not similarly provided for.

I hate everything about that.
I just want to see the whole world
whole.

IN THE MIDDLE OF THE AIR

Come and meet me in
the middle of the air
the song refrains, only
it is hard to sing out
your intentions when
your timeline has been compressed
from T H I S to
this.

His hand clutched ferociously
in yours, you both
weep salty tears and you
wrap one arm around his
shaking shoulders, at least until
he is willing to stand alone
again, which—he assures you—
he will be never, and that
is why you are both
crying.

TOMORROW VS. TODAY

Tomorrow and today do not
balance nicely on the scales
of decision-making, holding
in one hand the carpe diem
and in the other attempting
to seize something of the future
in order to make a future-you
proud.

What is joy today worth
measured against satisfaction
tomorrow? Surely the ant
and the grasshopper have different
answers when it comes to this,
and although we are trained
in matters fabulous to prize
the ant, when it comes to
terminal illness the credence
falls weightier to the grasshopper.

What then, when one is waiting
for a miracle? How much
does investment in one's future
correlate to
joy lived in the moment, if that
investment also brings joy but
could prove little more return;
if the future is abbreviated,

bringing with it
costly events we wish rather
to avoid? How much
is a pricey class taken now,
expected to bear fruit in months
or years to come, against the
potential of a single income labouring
under the weight of bills yet unreduced
if the worst should befall?

A class seems innocent, mayhaps,
but there *is* a line, somewhere
out there beyond our daily memento
mori, a point at which a yacht today
or never more attending work or school
becomes not seizing days, but
rather begging
for houselessness or hunger.
Where then the line, tomorrow vs.
today, hung weighty on the ever-
swinging scales?
Therein, perhaps, the answer:
vacillation.
In every moment, the balance due
that time, and every moment falling
to ant or hopper according
to its rhyme.

REBIRTH IS INEVITABLE

Children scream and
laughing shrieks echo off tiled
walls, bouncing through the space
like tiny rubber balls that splash
as they land in the gently shifting,
chlorine-scented, ocean made miniature
to contain its glory while
excluding all things inhuman.

Serious swimmers to the back, please,
where icy waters wait to welcome
sweat-soaked muscles slicing silently
through laborious lap lanes, where
swimmers stroke back and forth,
back and forth, back
and forth.

In the middle, the older folk and
rehab crew, water lapping at their
waists as they lap the waist-deep
water in their own way: crab-walking,
backwards-walking, wandering
meanderingly if that's the most they can manage,
moving muscles made for motion but
which age or injury or sheer bad luck or
different causes of different abilities have
meant the lap pool isn't for them.

At the front, the delighted screaming of
children small through large, splashing,
stamping, semi-submerged like cruising
sharks looking for a place to happen, and
the ring of fountains gently warming
patient watchers, guardians, the fountains
sentinels to it all.

The water cascading down from them onto
exposed backs and tired shoulders and necks
bent from the weight of watchful care is
a baptism, because that's
what water is for.
Whether shower, swimming pool or
fount, the purpose is the same: to cleanse
away our fears and soothe
away our sooted souls,
leaving them fresh-laundered
and powder-scented, chlorinated free
of all contamination, anything inhuman,
sparkling bright in sunshine that
plays off water drops like
spotlights, gleaming gold and
precious onto that which matters most.

To enter the water is to be
reborn, in some shape
or another, inevitably.

POEMS AND OCEANS BOTH ENCIRCLE THE WORLD

Another poem has occurred,
as is their wont, and
as words trickle from my soul,
down through my arms into my
fragile fingertips, like the blood of
life that pumps my thoughts and
makes crimson with life the very
essence of my body, I am once again
changed.
Transformed, if that's not too grand a word
for what is, really, a quite mundane process,
one that occurs whenever our hearts
meet fiction or story, fable or song that stirs
the very recesses of our identity,
affirming that which we love most about
ourselves or else challenging us
to greater heights.

Poetry flows like the sea, in and out, in
and out, a gentle tidal assault assuaging
all our guilt, soothing all our fears,
providing space in which to bathe and
re-emerge, cleansed and new, salt-skinned and
crusty-haired, a look which oughtn't be

aesthetic and yet somehow, inevitably,
is.
Perhaps because we see and value
the transformation that occurs within, and thus
are willing to put aside any constructed social
notions of beauty and aesthetic, gripped by
something far more primal, far more raw,
something transcendental as we recognise
in beach-salted waves of hair and tangled,
knotted fingers that work to smooth the
sand from sunburned skin our true
humanity, birthed from the sea.

As the ocean, thus poetry; in and out, in
and out, and we are left salt-crusted, and
even when we don't quite understand the
voice the ocean speaks with, the words unspooling
line by line like waves, in and out, in
and out, still we recognise that glint in our eyes
that means that transformation has occurred,
like poetry,
inevitably.

THE VALUE WE ATTRIBUTE

Today, I need you to know that
usually, if you are patient,
things tend to work out alright.
I'm not referring to the things
we can't control, of course,
the acts of God so called because
they lie far outside our grasp, their
causation dwelling somewhere out there
in the spinning of star-spangled space,
beyond the comprehension
of even our wisest of sages.
No.
I'm speaking instead of something
just as vast, just as unexplored, just as
deep,
but something over which we have
as much control as we should care to mine,
digging ever downward into
shafts sculpted from sweat, and blood, and
memory, nothing less than our identity
sparkling through veins in the rock of the walls,
becoming ever clearer as we approach—
asymptote-like—
the motherlode.

Weirdly, this is a poem about food.

I have transformed.

In the act of digging down deep into dark
recesses of my dust-worn soul, I sought a sense
of peace to quell this restless hatred I had
devised against the act of physical nourishment,
one whereby any act of consumption—the
necessary kind, the kind that is sustainable because
its function is to sustain—felt grotesque, unbearable,
a flowchart fraught with failure—a mine,
in fact, overrun with ends bluntly
dead, where any
answer I might craft was ipso facto
wrong.

But, in so digging, deep down into the depths
of psychological wells, in search of any glimmering
thread I might pull to untangle the whys and wheretofores
of this unnecessary angst, I did indeed strike gold:
The gold of saffron-flavoured rice, steamed gently
on the stove; the gold of olive oil, pouring like blessings
from a cold, darkened bottle from the farm; the gold
of yellow potatoes and sautéed onions and garlic crushed
until its heady fragrance fills the air and we
salivate in heady expectation.

In mining deep, I have found once more the joy,
like gem-filled geodes gashed to reveal
crystals to the light, that is possible in the
simple alchemy of the kitchen, and although
my countertops in actuality clutter with
crusted crockery and dirty detritus,
deep in the recesses of my soul they shine
like the promise of an alchemical
find.

Gold has its uses, to be sure, but in the end,
it's only worth the value we assign.

WELTSCHMERZ II

The face I pull as salty
tears track down my cheeks in
snail-lines of silver will never
be as ugly as the world,
which is full of burnished bronzed
slashes of anger and rage, bullets
blossoming into flowers the colour
of fire and fear, where difference
is greater than the sum of all parts and
I am at a loss
for how to curate
my damns.

Hope germinates in the dark but
a seed planted too deeply just
dies.

I have nothing to offer except words.

I have nothing to offer except
words which seem frail and futile,
words which others have spoken plenty before,
words which, if they were truly to be
of any use, would have been so before now.

Hope germinates in the dark.

The pea seeds I planted last month, one
third of them have come up, frail fronds
unfolding upright through the soil that
sustains them, from dark into light where
sprouts unfurl into blossoms the colour
of peace.
Are the rest dead, or do they merely
take their time?

Hope germinates in the dark.
One wonders what the germination rate
will be.

BECAUSE STORIES MATTER

*Nothing dies
when everything is connected.* - Danica Boyce

We have been un-Earthed.
We have been un-Earthed by greed and
the quest for power and
the way that this has been transmuted into
patriarchy, racial supremacy, imperialism,
colonisation; any other -ism or -ation or -arcy that seeks to set
one subgroup of humanity atop
another.

And this is our un-Earthing: a fundamental
dis
-connect
with things physical and dark, feminine and
feeling, things Earthy, here-and-now, not
then-and-yet-to-come.

One day, we may reach our former life.
One day, we may reach our forward life.
But mindfulness—the kind that is not
demure but rather
screams with joy into the living moment,
the shout of defiance that signals

I am
the present connection of infinitesimal
depth with the sunshine surrounding
our hearts—*that* mindfulness
demands the present be a gift worthy
of some as-yet-indefinable future.

We have become un-Earthed, because
our vision is toward the stars, and
while forests shatter from their heights and
rivers evaporate from their lowlands we
stare outward, focused
on the glitter of yet-to-come, and
this is a disservice to us all, for
even if the yet-to-come *does* come—
inevitably, it comes for us all, and
a thief in the night comes only to take
that which has value
(this present darkness must therefore
be worth the stealing, and mindfulness,
the kind that is not demure, must
agree)—it does not
serve us to be un-Earthed by
-isms that dis-
connect us from ourselves.

We only reach the future by
wading through the now.
Even if this is all a dream, thought
up by a universe whose galaxies spiral
in precisely the same arrangement as
the neurons that invoke thoughts our own,
even if the inevitable inevitably arrives and
reveals itself to contain Something More,

even then, the present is not to be
bypassed away.
Even if this is all a story...
Well.
We've all read stories; we know why they
exist.
Thousands of millennia of humanity and
stories are still the best way we have
of making people
care.

SORROW IS NOT INHERENTLY GREATER

(To every English faculty alive)

I think there is no magic
in sadness that allows us to transmute
it into art.

I think that, despite the heart-buoying
joy of happy moments, these lack magic
also.

Either are just as likely to inspire art, and
thus we must allow that either
there is magic in them both, or else
the magic lies elsewhere—in the wielder.

The gift of sorrow may indeed
be an outpouring of transmutational
artistry, and that is compensation;
but just as equally many
suffer
and make no art to pay for it.

That sorrow is somehow *more*
shows—to me—a kind of
refusal,
a denial,

of the incontrovertible truth:
That sorrows come, and they are
raw, but that does not ipso
facto make them
noble, and certainly not more noble
than plain old
incontrovertible
joy.

DECOMPRESSION

The table is covered in clutter and
I am drowning in watercolour paints and
piles of discarded brushes, clean and dirty, and
the pink paint bucket is full of old, stale water
tinged brownish grey by the mingling
of many paints and
there are stacks of paper, some fresh, pristine,
pressed flat in pads of potential, some
warped by watery use, wearing the colours
of creativity in languid lines or bold
brush strokes, and the wooden chair
(mango) is stacked higher than
the table with pink-and-teal journals and
hardback books containing creativity and crafts and
a teetering pile of boxes boasts pompom
beasts and crochet bunnies and scratch art
ready for the scratching.
Somewhere in the midst of all this mess,
pot plants thrive, long having outlived their
expected expiration date, in pots of
cream and charcoal and baby pink.
The table is covered with a raggy blue beach towel
that could be said to have seen better days, except
which is better, really: to towel down bodies
crispy with sea salt and toasted by the sun,
fresh from the waves, encrusted by sand,
or to bear witness to spontaneous creation,

the act of bringing something forth from nothing, with nothing more than kinetic energy, colour and potential?
Trick question, of course: they are both delightful.

A TRANSLATION FROM GIF TO POETRY, FROM GIFS ARRANGED IN RESPONSE TO POETRY

With a million thanks to Jessica, not just for this, but everything

But I just let my hands
make what they want to make,
he says, precision brush in hand,
eyes fixed on the intricacies of
his terracotta fish as he explains the simple
magic of creativity for the camera
(and that is truth, for hands will make
what hands will make, whether we
will it or no).

It's scary—both the world, and the idea that
we have little control, in the end, over what
our hands and hearts decide to make, or
at least far littler control than
we would wish to believe—but hey.
At least there's arts and crafts, a tiny
moment of rebellion against a world that
would rather consume our soul.

Pusheen, of course, understands: the artistic
path is really, at its heart, one of conquering
that fear, of finding one's way out
of the cycle that is idea—new supplies—
butt up against the concrete wall of
learning something new—depart to find
another wall that seems much easier to scale.
(We know, however, that the grass is greenest
where you water it, or perhaps where something
died; so too with walls, no matter how high
and impassable they appear.)

The simple joy of good markers, rainbow.

Creativity is what will set you free in
the end, and

watercolour lines and
tangled Celticesque patterns and
berries blue blooming from the tips of your brushes
like promises blooming into water
make the struggle all
worthwhile.

A CONCLUSION OF SORTS

It is cheap to say I'm enjoying my life
when blood tests bear testament to healing and
energy levels improve now week on week,
but it has nevertheless cost me to be here, so
I hope you will forgive me when I say,
If this is the Rubicon I had to cross
to reach the promised land,
so be it.

ABOUT THE AUTHOR

AMY LAURENS is an Australian author of fantasy fiction for all ages. Her story *Bones Of The Sea*, about creepy carnivorous mist and bone curses, won the 2021 Aurealis Award for Best Fantasy Novella.

Amy has also written the award-winning portal-fantasy *Sanctuary* series about Edge, a 13-year-old girl forced to move to a small country town because of witness protection (the first book is *Where Shadows Rise*), the humorous fantasy *Kaditeos* series, following newly graduated Evil Overlord Mercury as she attempts to acquire a castle, the young adult series *Storm Foxes*, about love and magic and family in small town Australia, and a whole host of non-fiction.

Head to www.AmyLaurens.com to find out more!

Read more by Amy Laurens!

poems of becoming

CHANGE BECOMES US

AMY LAURENS
Aurealis Award-winning author

www.ingramcontent.com/pod-product-compliance
Lightning Source LLC
Chambersburg PA
CBHW060340080526
44584CB00013B/853